THE
POTENT FORCE
OF SPONSORSHIP

OMO-OJO ERNEST IVIE

The Potent Force of Sponsorship

© 2017, Omo-Ojo Ernest Ivie

Researched and written by Omo-Ojo Ernest Ivie

omoojoivie@gmail.com

ISBN: 978-978-960-650-4

Designed by Phrik Design Abuja, 08175855947, phrikdesign@gmail.com

Printed & bound in Nigeria

ENDORSEMENTS:

The raw passion, energy, resilience and "can do" spirit that have characterized Ivie's life and work flows through this book!

The easy flow and prosaic smoothness equally describes the reality of the life of the writer. All of these is strengthened by the eternal truth of the word of God which Ivie himself has allowed to guide his life as a young man.

Simply put, this work is a foretaste of greater creative and narrative works that I am certain we will see from Ivie in the near future.

I absolutely recommend this book for all young men and women who are ready to take on life!

Regards,

Adedayo (Dayo) Ojo

CEO Caritas Communications, Lagos, Nigeria

ENDORSEMENTS:

Omo-Ojo Ernest Ivie has created a masterpiece in the potent force of sponsorship. With scriptural support and practical encounters, Ivie shows us who your sponsor is in life and provides a practical guide in identifying your mentor and your sponsor. This book is a reality of our time, our walk with God and mankind. Ivie is the dawning of a new phase in your purpose on earth.

Well done Ivie.

Hendricks Echoga

(Serving Overseer)

Revival Bible Ministries, F.C.T. Abuja, Nigeria

ENDORSEMENTS:

I have read some chapters of this book and find it quite revealing and hard to put down once you start! In the book, Ernest approaches the subject matter from three broad perspectives -

His personal life experiences, General practical application from his observations as well as from events in Scripture.

He also makes the distinction between Sponsors and Mentors very clear and beneficial for youths, making it a practical guide.

I therefore recommend the book as very beneficial for everyone, especially those who aspire to excel in life and need guidance.

Elaye Otrofanowei

CEO, Swift Car Rental, Lagos, Nigeria

TO GLORIA..

..the love of my life. Popularly known as 'Ukinebo', my rising star. I call her the 'complete package' Thanks for believing in me even when no other person took notice. You are my love, a dear friend, and I would not have been who I am today without your encouraging words constantly giving that push to excel to the next level.

You are not only an incredibly beautiful woman; you are also very attractive. Not all beautiful women are attractive; I respect you and do look forward to spending the rest of our lives together.

TO IWINOSA

My sweet and lovely daughter. You are not only beautiful on the outside, but also on the inside, smart, intelligent, soft spoken, kind, compassionate and with a heart of gold.

I am your number one fan and I will always love you.

TO DIVINE

Divine my son, like momma will always call you. You possess the zest of energy and with you there are no dull moments. No wonder I call you Osawemwenhio - God has caused me to brag in Him.

As your name is, so shall your life be, you will possess the gates of your enemies and your generation will call you blessed. I see you as one of the upcoming computer wizards of this millennium.

Daddy loves you.

TABLE OF CONTENTS

Sponsor: Life without a sponsor cannot reach its zenith. Most times we tend to confuse our mentor with our sponsor, but the truth is that they are different and each plays a distinctive role in our lives.

INTRODUCTION

Life without a sponsor cannot reach its zenith. Most times we tend to confuse our mentor with our sponsor, but the truth is that they are both different and each plays a distinctive role in our life.

The most common practice is that we generally place too much attention on mentorship and discard the most useful of the success chain, which is the sponsor. In fact, a sponsor is more critical than a mentor. Ask yourself of what use is all the coaching and mentoring if you do not have a platform to showcase all you have learnt.

In this book, I will attempt to explain the following key concepts, postulations and much more:

- Who is a Sponsor?

- Why do we need a Sponsor?

- Can you reach your zenith without a Sponsor?

- Do we confuse a Mentor with a Sponsor?

- If you expect a mentor to play the role of sponsor, it comes with frustration, anger and hatred

- Does the world run on sponsorship?

- Your hate or dislike for this principle will not make it go away- some people call this *'ojoro'* or favouritism

- Businesses/corporate world run on this principle

- Entertainment industry runs on this principle

- Churches or religious organisations run on this principle

- Politicians use this principle

- Sportsmen use this principle- some call them agents or scouts

- Is it scriptural and spiritual?

The desire to write this book was borne out of a drive to showcase a personal account of a man who has benefited enormously from the sponsorship principle. If it worked for me, it can also work for you, it is a universal principle. Principles do not discriminate on the basis of colour, race, tribe or religion. If you follow the principle, it will work for you.

My experience in my career as an intern serving in my present organisation, which eventually employed me three years after I completed my internship, is a demonstration of the power of sponsorship.

I recalled while serving as an intern in my organisation as Abuja liaison officer, my primary job was to support very senior company executives. Key amongst these roles was to support the Managing Director.

Looking back, I can say I did my assigned job diligently and with all the passion it deserved. One remarkable experience I can recall was my being noticed by a federal minister then, Admiral Jubrilla Ayinla (Rtd.). This minister took a liking for me and my passion for the job, such that during the period of my internship he personally wrote two recommendation letters to both my Managing Director and the then company Vice-Chairman, paying glowing tributes to my talent and skill in executing my job. He further endorsed me and recommended that the company should look at a possible opportunity of offering me a long-term career.

This was sponsorship at play, I had never met this federal minister before then, but he took notice of me any time I accompanied my managing director to meetings with him as it was within my job description to set up those meetings.

Guess what? Nothing happened immediately after I completed my internship. However, I continued doing my job to the best of my ability as a contract-hire for about three years after I completed my internship. the Managing Director was very instrumental to my eventual hire as a permanent employee.

In fact, according to the account I was told by my manager then, the Managing

Director was so focused with my being hired, that he personally ensured it was one of the last assignments he had to do before retiring from the company in the year 2000.

Today, looking back, I am eternally grateful to that first sponsorship endorsement I got from Admiral Ayinla, which was to set up a chain of events that were to follow in the course of my career and life.

1
WHO IS A SPONSOR?

The origin of the word 'Sponsor' dates back to the mid-17th century. It started as a noun from the Latin 'spondere', which translates into 'promise solemnly.' The verb form of Sponsor dates from the late 19th century.

Sponsors provide funds for a project or activity or the person carrying it out, for example, when someone 'is being sponsored by his church'. The word sponsor could also mean to introduce and support (a proposal) in a legislative assembly: for example, "Senator Divine sponsored the bill."

According to Merriam Webster, Sponsor means one who presents a candidate for baptism or confirmation and undertakes responsibility for the person's religious education or spiritual welfare. It could also mean one who assumes responsibility for some other person or thing or alternative.

Dictionary.com defines Sponsor variously as "a person who vouches or is responsible for a person or thing; a person, firm, organisation, etc., that finances and buys the time to broadcast a radio or television program so as to advertise a product, a political party, etc.; a person who makes a pledge or promise on behalf of another; a person who answers for an infant at baptism, making the required professions and assuming responsibility for the child's religious upbringing; godfather or godmother."

A sponsor is a person or an organization that pays for or plans and carries out a project or activity; and finally, a sponsor is one that pays the cost of a radio or television program, usually in return for advertising time during its course.

What is 'Corporate Sponsorship'?

A corporate sponsorship is a form of marketing in which a corporation pays for all or some of the costs associated with a project or program in exchange for recognition. Corporations may have their logos and brand names displayed alongside those of the organization undertaking the project or program, with specific mention that the corporation has provided funding.

Corporate sponsorships are commonly associated with non-profit groups, which generally would not be able to fund operations and activities without outside financial assistance. It is not the same as philanthropy.

Marketing terms.com defines Sponsorship as Advertising that seeks to establish a deeper association and integration between an advertiser and a publisher, often involving coordinated beyond-the-banner placements.

Life without a sponsor cannot reach his zenith. Most times we tend to confuse our mentor with our sponsor, but the truth is that they are both different and each plays a distinct role in our life. In fact, a sponsor is more critical than a mentor.

What I find most striking in all the early and contemporary definitions of the word sponsor is that it started as a noun in the 17th century but its form changed in the 19th century when it became a verb. My elementary understanding of English says verb is an action word.

There is also a clear distinction from the words sponsorship and philanthropy, which means that sponsorship does not happen by accident. It is deliberate, thought over, planned and executed. It takes a lot for someone to agree to undertake a sponsorship; it demands responsibility from both partners. Most times the person sponsoring must find value before embarking on the mission. It does not come cheap, it is expensive and as such you have to earn it, there are no emotions about it, which is why it is not a philanthropic movement.

Qualities of a sponsor:

- Announces your arrival to the stage

- Makes room for you

- Sponsors are very impatient and very strategic

- They are visionary- they see opportunities well ahead

- They usually have big egos

- They could charge a fee

- They could demand rewards

- They do not operate based on emotions

Interestingly, what I have found out in the course of research and life experiences is that people tend to confuse these two roles. Some people once they identify a mentor they are caught in the web of expectation that the mentor would place them on the world map. This is not the modus operandi.

Interestingly, what I have found out in the course of research and life experiences is that people tend to confuse these two roles. Some people once they identify a mentor they are caught in the web of expectation that the mentor would place them on the world map. This is not the modus operandi.

2

SPONSOR VS
MENTORS

A sponsor is distinctively different from a mentor and they both play different roles in our lives.

Mentor:

A mentor is someone inside or outside your organisation who can give advice, feedback and encouragement. Think of people within your field whom you admire.

- Within your organisation who might provide perspective and counsel you on your organisation's unwritten rules

- Outside your organisation, who might provide guidance in your field and help your career.

Sponsor:

A sponsor is someone within or outside your organisation who has positional and political influence to help you move your career or life forward. Sponsors provide leads to advancement and growth.

I once had a young pastor friend growing and serving as an assistant pastor in a city where I used to live. This pastor was so good that he also doubled as the personal assistant to the bishop.

At some point in this pastor's life he desired a move and an upliftment, which is typical of a young man aspiring for growth. His desire was very legitimate but, guess what, he was looking up to the Bishop for that upliftment. The only error was that the Bishop was his mentor and not his sponsor.

In frustration, this pastor came to me for support and counsel. I asked him to send me his profile and I decided to package this young pastor and sold him to higher influential authorities, bigger than his local bishop. I sustained this recommendation with phone calls, text messages and emails showcasing values this young pastor would bring to the church organization if he were given that platform.

Don't waste your time and energy on people who would not celebrate you, look for people who believe in you and in your vision.

The good news is that my push paid off and in a short time, this young pastor was posted to one of the south-south states in Nigeria to go head the work there and he's doing great work there today.

So, the admonition is, we must be able to separate these roles. Someone may love you, but that does not necessarily translate to him speaking for you when opportunities beckon. Don't waste your time and energy on people who would not celebrate you, look for people who believe in you and in your vision.

Your sponsor may even be a Muslim and you are a Christian, your sponsor may be your boss's driver or cook. Keep your eyes open, ears on red alert, do not discriminate, you can never tell who will speak for you, all that is required is to be sensitive.

Develop your network; construct your own personal developmental network of people inside and outside your workplace, church or community.

The world runs on sponsorship; so, do not treat it with kid gloves. You can never get to your zenith without a sponsor. A mentor is good, but having a good mentor without a sponsor is time and energy wasted.

The world is waiting to celebrate you, but we all need a platform. Guess what, we don't need more than a platform; just one opportunity and the rest is history. Consider great talents in sports, music, entertainment that we may never see or hear from because they were not given that opportunity. This is what I mean by sponsorship.

The world runs on sponsorship; so, do not treat it with kid gloves. You can never get to your zenith without a sponsor. A mentor is good, but having a good mentor without a sponsor is time and energy wasted.

Don't be selfish and self-serving; even if you have to pay a sponsor, go ahead and cut a deal. Sponsorships are not for free they cost something; you must be prepared to pay for it. This is why you see entertainers change their sponsors, they are permanently looking for the best deal; there are no emotions to it.

Don't be selfish and self-serving, even if you have to pay the sponsor, go ahead and cut a deal. Sponsorships are not for free, they cost something; you must be prepared to pay for it. This is why you see entertainers change their sponsors, they are permanently looking for the best deal; there are no emotions to it.

3

SPONSORSHIP VALIDATIONS-BIBLICAL ILLUSTRATIONS

In This chapter, I would attempt to demonstrate that the world runs on sponsorship and also show scenarios with spiritual examples to support my postulation.

Jesus & John the Baptist

Jesus is our greatest example in the bible. Did Jesus have a sponsor? The answer is yes. John the Baptist was the sponsor of Jesus. Almighty God knew how key this principle was and had to ensure that John the Baptist was conceived six months ahead of the conception of Jesus Christ.

Jesus endorsed the sponsorship principle in John 5: 31-32, thus: 'if I testify about myself, my testimony is not valid. There is another who testifies in my favour and I know that his testimony about me is valid.'

John announced the arrival of Jesus to the scene; in fact before JESUS appeared, he was already talking and singing his praises — 'there is one coming whose shoes am not worthy to unloose, he shall baptise you with the Holy Ghost and with fire.'

'If I testify about myself, my testimony is not valid. There is another who testifies in my favour and I know that his testimony about me is valid.'

When Jesus finally appeared, John announced his arrival, saying: 'behold the Lamb of God which taketh away the sins of the World.' In fact, he went further to say, 'He will increase and I will decrease.' This was, and still is, the most powerful statement made by any man on planet earth. No wonder Christ said of all men born of women no one is as great as John. He was the star sponsor of the age, because he unselfishly announced the entry of Jesus to the scene and he stepped aside.

> *'He will increase and I will decrease.' This was and still is the most powerful statement made by any man on planet earth. No wonder Christ said of all men born of women no one is as great as John. He was the star sponsor of the age, because he unselfishly announced the entry of Jesus to the scene and he stepped aside.*

Guess what, as typical of most sponsors, he wanted to get a reward. Was he wrong to expect that? After his arrest by Herod, he expected Jesus to come and secure his release and in the process, he got frustrated and sent messages to Jesus.

Then he asked of Jesus, are you the one we are expecting or do we have to wait again? This was the error of John the Baptist when he found himself in a very frustrating situation. Jesus in response sent a message, telling his disciples to inform him of the testimonies that were happening. John never came out of that arrest, he died with his head chopped off.

David & Jonathan

Another biblical illustration of a sponsor was the story of David and Jonathan. Jonathan loved David like his own soul. He announced David to the main stage and was prepared to sacrifice his kingship for David. He introduced David to the palace and the inner workings of the environment in preparation of things to come.

He brought credible intelligence to David, and on several occasions, he saved David from danger. We all need a Jonathan in our life; no one can arrive the scene without a sponsor. Life is in stages and men are in sizes.

'The race is not for the swift, the battle is not for strong, but time and chance happened to them all.' David knew how key Jonathan was to his emergence as King, that even after Jonathan died in battle, David knew he had a debt to pay.

David looked earnestly for someone from Jonathan's loins. He said is 'there no person of this household I can bless?' Finally, after much search he was told there was a man, but the news was that he was lame.

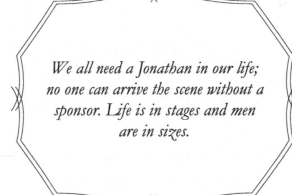

We all need a Jonathan in our life; no one can arrive the scene without a sponsor. Life is in stages and men are in sizes.

When Mephibosheth was a child, while war raged in grandfather Saul's house, his nurse picked him up to safety as the enemy came to destroy the entire household. While the nurse was running with him, he fell and Mephibosheth sustained an injury, which made him to become lame.

David sent emissaries to go fetch Mephibosheth and David blessed him and made him to live in the king's palace and all his descendants.

Moses & Pharaoh's Daughter

The story of Moses and pharaoh's daughter - a biblical classical example of a sponsor at birth that was divinely orchestrated.

Moses was born at a time in Egypt when there was a decree that all male Hebrew children under the age of three should be killed. But God brought a sponsor in the person of pharaoh's daughter. She saw Moses and instantly took an interest in him and took Moses from the bank of the Nile River to the palace.

There were other Hebrew male children born about this same time, but the account was that they all fell prey of this draconian law. The grace Moses enjoyed was that a sponsor showed up, who not only spoke for him, but paid the price to have him nurtured.

She knew instantly that Moses was potentially destined to be great. She took him home, got him a nurse and had Moses trained as a Prince in the house of Pharaoh. Moses grew and became the great deliverer God used to rescue the Hebrew nation from captivity in Egypt into the land of promise.

There are times in our life, either in our work place or in our family, when our head is about to be chopped off, due to some misguided information about us, or just that we were at the wrong place, the defining moment for us at this point is for a sponsor to show up.

General Naaman and the Jewish Maid

Let us look at the story of the Aram general by name Naaman (2 Kings 5:1-26) who was a leper, and had tried all means to get well but was not feasible. The bible account had it that a sponsor came in the person of a young Jewish girl who was captured as one of the spoils of war and was living with this general as a maid.

Guess what, which Sponsor did Jesus leave us with? The Holy Spirit. The bible calls the Holy Spirit our greatest advocate. The Holy Spirit is the greatest sponsor of all time. The Holy Spirit intercedes for us. Power only came to the disciples after the Holy Spirit arrived the scene, and ordinary men became extraordinary men and all marveled at the transformation that happened.

This miracle was almost aborted, because General Naaman had gone to his master the King of Aram for a recommendation letter to be written by him to the King of Israel. King talking to King *abi*? The process almost ended in fiasco, probably Naaman must have despised the instruction of the little maid, but the charge from her was clear: 'go and meet Prophet Elisha, no intermediary.'

The account had it that she encouraged her boss to go and see prophet Elisha and that he would be made whole. The circumstances did not play out as the General expected, his desire was that the prophet would come out and receive him as an important VIP, but the bible account was the prophet simply passed a message through his staff Gehazi, that Naaman should go to River Jordan and wash seven times and he would be fine.

Initially he got infuriated at the directive of the prophet, but after much admonition from his servant he obeyed. And then came the defining moment of his life - immediately he dipped the seventh time and came out, his body we are told became as that of a little child. A sponsor showing up as a maid. Think about that.

Jesus recognised the power and potency of this principle that even after his death and resurrection, He said 'I would not leave you comfortless.' He told his disciples to tarry in Jerusalem until they were endued with power from on high.

Guess what, which Sponsor did Jesus leave us with? The Holy Spirit. The bible calls the Holy Spirit our greatest advocate. The Holy Spirit is the greatest sponsor of all time. The Holy Spirit intercedes for us. Power only came to the disciples after the Holy Spirit arrived the scene, and ordinary men became extraordinary men and all marveled at the transformation that happened.

Do you have a sponsor today? If not, you must get one or put yourself in place to be discovered by a sponsor.

The question is, when the opportunity presents itself, are you ready to seize the stage and the momentum? It is the duty of the sponsor to create the scene and open the platform, but you must take the opportunity and maximise it, which is why you must get ready. Prepare yourself for the opportunities to come, develop both your soft and hard skills.

The battle of life is first won in the mind. What your heart can't handle, your hand will not be able to. You must visualize a mental map and where you desire to be and believe in your heart that it is possible.

The question is, when the opportunity presents itself, are you ready to seize the stage and the momentum? It is the duty of the sponsor to create the scene and open the platform, but you must take the opportunity and maximise it, which is why you must get ready. Prepare yourself for the opportunities to come, develop both your soft and hard skills.

Rebecca & Jacob

The story of Rebecca and Jacob, Gen. 27:5-30. Rebecca took the biggest risk for her son Jacob, as failure to deliver could have placed a curse on her son. In Gen. 27:13, his mother said 'let the curse fall on me, just do what I say, go and get them for me.'

This was a classical illustration of two

brothers both born same day and to the same parents. In fact account had it that Esau came out first and was therefore the first born by right. He was also the beloved of the father, so nature was on his side.

But at the defining moment when transfer of power was to happen, even though he was clearly in the advantage he lost out. The only issue was that he had no sponsor. Jacob had the advantage that was clearly created by his mother.

The sponsor came with a strategy, which reduced time and made resources available, so efficiency was at play here, as time was of essence and so before Esau came back all was done and dusted. This is what sponsors bring to the table. Your journey of a thousand miles can be reduced to a day's journey.

> *The sponsor came with a strategy, which reduced time and made resources available, so efficiency was at play here, as time was of essence and so before Esau came back all was done and dusted. This is what sponsors bring to the table. Your journey of a thousand miles can be reduced to a day's journey.*

Sponsors take the blow for you and make their resources available for your use, that way you maximise time and leverage on that platform. We all need leveraging, don't despise the power of leveraging, it's the difference why two people who set out on the same journey same day to the same destination arrive differently.

In life, overtaking is allowed in the course of events. No wonder there was an account when David returned from battle and his enemies had taken all the wives and children of Israel into captivity. David was very disenchanted and the people made to stone him, but David enquired of the Lord if he should pursue and if there were chances he would still meet up.

The account had it that the Lord told him to go and that he will not only overtake the enemies but will without fail recover all, and that was precisely what happened.

A sponsor sees what you do not see and is prepared to take risks on your behalf. In fact, after the blessing 'theft' was executed and Esau came charging to snuff the life out of Jacob, Rebecca also made a way of escape for Jacob to run to her brother Laban.

Joseph & the Cupbearer

The turning point for Joseph moving from

prison to becoming the prime minister in Egypt was his profiling by the cupbearer. Joseph had a chance meeting with the cupbearer in prison and interpreted his dreams and in fact asked that the cupbearer remember him when he is restored to his job in the palace.

> *Truth of the matter was that Potiphar was not joseph's sponsor; he was merely a mentor to prepare him for the job to come. When the sponsor finally showed up in the person of the cupbearer, the story changed.*

History recorded that the cupbearer completely forgot Joseph for almost 2 years until Pharaoh dreamt. That was when the cupbearer spoke in glowing terms about the qualities of Joseph in interpreting dreams, and Pharaoh asked that Joseph be brought out of prison and that was the road to his making as Egyptian prime minister (Gen. 41).

Something very interesting about the life of Joseph - just before he was thrown into prison, he served Potiphar, a man who was very senior in Pharaoh's palace. Now ask yourself, how come the recommendation for his uplift never came from Potiphar? The bible account had it that his boss was so pleased with his delivery that he made him a captain over his entire household.

Truth of the matter was that Potiphar was not Joseph's sponsor; he was merely a mentor to prepare him for the job to come. When the sponsor finally showed up in the person of the cupbearer, the story changed.

In life, so many of us make this mistake of fixing our eyes on people we think would introduce us to the scene, we must be sensitive enough to know and be able to decipher if truly they are our sponsor.

The account about Joseph and this man was very revealing, this was the only man he met who actually told him to remember him. What this tells me was that Joseph knew this man was very strategic in the dynamics of the palace. Even though he had a temporary setback, Joseph knew he would be back to reckoning and he quickly tried to extract a commitment. Destiny helpers always will show up, the big question, would you know when they arrive the scene?

Ruth & Naomi

This account is recorded in Ruth Chapter 2. Naomi can be considered the sponsor of

Ruth. This was a story about a mother in law and a daughter in law. After the death of her husband, Ruth returned with Naomi to the land of Canaan.

Ruth had all the right reasons to despise this woman, given the account that she lost her three sons, including Ruth's husband. The natural feeling in today's world is that this woman (Naomi) is a bad omen. But Ruth saw in this woman something that the other two daughters-in-law did not see, no wonder they both returned back to their country and she alone proceeded and followed.

Don't despise your destiny – helper, the person may show up in a manner you do not expect. Naomi's circumstances did not look wonderful but she had the key to unlock the future of Ruth. Ruth recognised this, no wonder despite all the pushbacks she got from Naomi that she should return to her country and people, she refused.

Consider this - are you sure Ruth did not have some pressure from the two other women (daughters-in-law) to follow them back? What about her own people - maybe father, mother, brothers and sisters - are you sure they did not also put pressure on her to not follow Naomi? But, against all odds, she stuck to her belief. Most times when you are taking that decision that could potentially change your destiny, you will be a loner, you may not have popular support.

I remember a personal account when I took the decision to get married October 10, 1998; it was a lonely decision. This was precisely 10 months after my National Youth Service Corps (NYSC). My family, friends, colleagues and associates felt I was just too young and with no experience, no stable job and regular income. But I was determined to prove that it was God's word for me, I did not allow my circumstance then to be sole determining factor for a life-long decision.

I took that leap of faith and today, 19 years after, I am blessed with two wonderful children - an undergraduate currently studying chemical engineering at A&M University, Houston, Texas, while the other just graduated from secondary school. God has truly blessed us. He took our feet from ground zero to surplus. If you dare to take that step of faith, God will definitely honour your faith.

The account had it that Naomi strategically positioned her daughter-in-law to be engaged to Boaz, as Ruth followed the script of Naomi to the latter. This union produced Obed. Obed was the father of Jesse and Jesse the father of David - what a process to the genealogy of Jesus, who is the lion of the tribe of Judah!

Saul- the first king of Israel

The potent force of sponsorship was at play in the making of the first king of Israel (1 Samuel 9: 6-20).

The story had it that Saul was asked by his father Kish to go look for a lost ass and Saul took along with him his servant. While in search of the ass they came to a town and his servant told him there was a prophet in that town, who happened to be Prophet Samuel. The servant counseled Saul that they should stop by and enquire from the prophet about the lost ass, as he had the power of a seer and could predict precisely where the ass could be found.

History recorded that Saul initially resisted, saying he had no gift to give the prophet but the servant said he had a gift and that he would make that available. This was sponsorship at play. Saul never knew destiny was waiting in the wings. At about that same hour, God had revealed to Prophet Samuel that a young man was coming to see him and that he should anoint him as the next king of Israel.

This chance meeting between Prophet Samuel and Saul, orchestrated by Saul's servant, would eventually lead to his making as the first king of Israel. You can never tell where your next breakthrough would come from, as the next person to you may just be the sponsor you have been waiting for, so do not despise small beginnings.

Jesus & the feeding of the 5000

An account is recorded in John 6: 1-10. This account recorded the feeding of five thousand people, excluding women and children.

You can never tell where your next breakthrough would come from, the next person to you may just be the sponsor you have been waiting for, so do not despise small beginnings.

Jesus was presented with a dilemma in the bush with no visible way of escape and, not willing to send the crowd away hungry, a sponsor came in the person of a little lad, who had five small barley loaves and two small fish. Jesus said this was more than enough. He lifted the items, prayed over them and commanded the disciples to share. The miraculous happened, as the whole crowd were fed and the disciples still had about loaded 12 baskets as left overs.

My puzzle for you about this account are: did this crowd of about five thousand men, excluding women and children, not have bread or fish of their own? Or had they eaten them before Jesus asked? How come a deliverer came in the person of a little lad?

Do not get yourself attached to people who are not prepared to make sacrifices, people who would eat their tomorrow today, people who would eat their seed and not wait for the harvest.

This little lad was strategic, he was probably listening with rapt attention to Jesus and forgot Mama gave him some stuff to eat. The adults probably instead of listening to Jesus were busy feasting on the takeaway they had for the trip.

Sponsors take risk, they are people who are ready to invest and wait for dividends. Impatient people who want instant rewards are no good sponsors.

This is why successful politicians are the ones with the long-vision approach to investment, people like Bola Tinubu, Atiku Abubakar, Ibrahim Babangida and Olusegun Obasanjo, among others - no wonder their relevance in the political terrain have stood the test of time.

This little lad was strategic, he was probably listening with rapt attention to Jesus and forgot Mama gave him some stuff to eat. The adults probably instead of listening to Jesus were busy feasting on the takeaway they had for the trip.

4

SPONSORSHIP
VALIDATIONS-
CONTEMPORARY
EXPERIENCES

Contemporary Sponsorships

This principle today defines the essence of politics, government, business, religion, entertainment, sports, etc. It is the single game changer or decider of who gets what, why, where and how. If you hate or fail to recognise and operate in this principle, your chances of succeeding and reaching your zenith are greatly diminished.

This game is about sponsorship, some people may call it recommendation; no matter the semantics, this is how the world operates. Man is a social being and what defines man and space is relationship.

One of the common sayings is that no man is an island. We are all products of connections and inter connections; we all, knowingly or unknowingly, are operating this principle, but you can only attract the best out of it if you become strategic in your approach.

Life can only give to you what you demand of it; after all, we are told that luck is only meaningful to a prepared man given an opportunity.

It is the single game-changer/decider of who gets what, why, where and how. If you hate or fail to recognise and operate in this principle your chances of succeeding and reaching your zenith is greatly diminished.

Archbishop Benson Idahosa can be classified as a big example of a modern day contemporary sponsor in the religious circle. This was a man of uncommon favour and ability - name it, there is virtually no big figure in the Christian religious body today that did not enjoy this man's sponsorship support.

Some men are kingmakers and this man of God arguably qualify as a generalissimo in this regard. Life without a sponsor cannot be fulfilled. Some sponsors have enriching capacities in creating multiple platforms; no wonder Papa Idahosa attracted so many people. People came from far and near to identify with him as he had that apostolic ministry to open doors beyond the unimaginable.

Every person, whether they were of his parent ministry or outside, who recognised this gift in this man of God and tapped into it had a turning experience. Papa Idahosa had the uncanny ability to open multiple platforms, such that today, close to 20 years after he passed on, his footprints are still in the sands of time.

Business Sponsorship:

This is the key principle that rules the business or corporate world. Those who move up the career ladder are not necessarily the hardest working in any organisation, but those who have positioned themselves and are able to operate on the basis of the sponsorship principle.

The name of the game is about positioning. There is just no way you can reach the zenith of your career without a sponsor. Ask yourself, who is there to speak for you when you are not there?

Guess what, when the issues of our lives are been discussed we are not there most of the time, a careless statement from someone at the decision point could just be the determining factor that may stop you from getting to the next level. Do you have sufficient network or someone who believes in you and is ready to take the blows on your behalf in defending you at the opportune time?

> *Life can only give to you, what you demand out of it; after all we are told that luck is only meaningful to a prepared man given an opportunity.*

Do not kid yourself and call it worshiping or praise - singing someone. I hear some people say 'I would not lick people's asses to get positions'; sorry, I have news for you, this is how the world operates - we all need a helping hand, don't be shy about it, it is not hero - worshiping, just do the right things and place yourself in a position to be discovered or admired by a sponsor.

No one can go on this journey of life alone, as there is a saying from back home where I come from that, there is no respect for a loner.

There are no self-made men, in fact the price to be a self-made man is too much of a burden to bear by one single person. The world is wired by sponsorships, why will you want to do it alone, just because you do not want to reference anyone on your journey to success?

This was the singular reason Satan failed and was thrown down from heaven by God, believing he could do everything by his own limited might. Any man without a reference or a story is a mysterious man,

God does not operate that way and neither do men.

Sports Sponsorship

This is the defining principle of the sports world; the name of the game is about sponsorships. The game is all about branding, advertising, packaging. This was why for decades Don King defined the essence of boxing. He is arguably the biggest promoter of boxing of this age.

You had to pay a price to be on his label, his games attracted the biggest appearance fee, he epitomised the word 'sponsorship' in the game of boxing and, guess what, he had no qualms about it - you hate him or love him at your own peril.

The games of soccer, tennis and athletics, for instance, are all defined by the essence of sponsorship. These sponsors are also known as agents or scouts. The value of your worth as a sportsman in determining what you get is not only based on your talent and skill, but equally on the manager you have, it is the scouts or agents that go in and do the hard bargaining for you.

Even though you have the talent, you cannot negotiate the best deal for yourself. Guess what, some of these agents charge very crazy fees, but if you choose to ignore them and say, 'well, I can do it on my own,' the chances of your succeeding are very limited.

Some sports folks have devised some smart ways of using a family member or friend as their sponsor, but the truth of the matter is that we all cannot deny the efficacy of having a sponsor, whatever the social relationship you have with that person. It defines the essence of the sports world.

These sponsors are also known as agent or scouts. The value of your worth as a sportsman in determining what you get is not only based on your talent and skill, but equally on the manager you have.

Political Sponsorship:

President Barak Obama's biggest leap in his political career was the one and only chance platform he had to present a speech at a Democrats convention. Someone introduced him and gave him that platform, and after he spoke the world discovered that there was a new star in the horizon waiting to be revealed.

That singular event set the scene for a series of quick events that followed: he transformed from being a junior ranking senator and contested to become the President of the United States of America and was elected the first black president to govern that great country.

Ask yourself, why would Asiwaju Bola Tinubu, a Muslim, sponsor Professor Yemi Osinbajo, of all the people he knew, when President Muhammadu Buhari needed a Christian as running mate during the 2015 elections? This relationship speaks volume about the person of Vice President Osinbajo. This is a classic modern-day sponsorship that played out in Nigeria in events leading to the 2015 presidential election.

When the Muslim - Muslim ticket presidential ambition could not be realised, President Buhari advised Asiwaju Tinubu to bring up a replacement. In fact history has revealed that Asiwaju Tinubu was asked to bring three names (see the book:

Against the Run of Play by Segun Adeniyi), but Asiwaju only gave one name, that of VP Osinbajo.

You must strive to get to a position where your sponsor will believe so much in you and would have no alternative to you, which speaks volume about loyalty and trust.

This principle is not *'ojoro'* (deceit), this is how the world operates and your feelings cannot change it. Instead of being frustrated by it, key into this principle.

> *This principle is not 'ojoro' (deceit), this is how the world operates and your feelings cannot change it. Instead of being frustrated by it, key into this principle.*

Entertainment Sponsorship:

In the entertainment world (or call it showbiz), the principle of sponsorship pervades all - artistes, actors, musicians, sculptors, writers, etc. - the buzzword is sponsorship.

A good musical success is not merely determined by how good the lyrics or how sonorous the voice of the singer is, but by its impact and impact translates to money and fame, among others. The only person that can determine the impact of music is not the singer, but the sponsor. No wonder, musicians or artistes all strive to be signed on by the biggest record label.

In fact, when you look at the operations of sponsorship in the entertainment world, you will be tempted to say the world is unfair, because it is not necessarily the best or most talented that rule the space; those who are making waves are those who enjoy the best projections. Some of the best-promoted and profitable songs contain lyrics that do not really make sense.

It is good to have the skills and raw talent, but ultimately your success and reach can only happen if you are given the platform and that can only happen with a sponsor.

Take a critical look at the top singers or musicians in the Nigerian music industry today, the only common denominator is their sponsor, the same is the case on the global scale. That is why some musicians go into what they call 'collabo' or collaboration, all part of the process of attracting the right sponsor and platform.

It is good to have the skills and raw talents, but ultimately your success and reach can only happen if you are given the platform and that can only happen with a sponsor.

5

SUMMARY &
CONCLUSION

We can only arrive the scene when a sponsor notices us. Look for your sponsor or put yourself in a position to be discovered by a sponsor. Some pointers to getting you ready to be discovered by a sponsor are:

- Develop your skills (both hard and soft skills)

- Humility to learn

- Patience

- Perseverance

- Loyalty

- Trust

Establishing a network is a matter of relationship-building over time. Always think of ways you can establish connections with people you would like to include in your network, such as a mentor and a sponsor. What steps can you take to get your network started? And what are the right conversations you might have?

Think of ways you can come into contact with people you want to get to know. How might you volunteer your time at work or in the local community? Are there affinity groups you can join? What social events can you attend? Can you reach out through social media? Can a mentor or a sponsor connect with you? Offering others a helping hand can also strengthen your network.

A personal brand is a shorthand expression of your strength and skills, it is the publicly acknowledged value you contribute. When it comes to growth in life, a positive personal brand is crucial. Leaders tend to consider people with positive personal brands to tap for a role or trust with a major account.

A personal brand is a shorthand expression of your strength and skills, it is the publicly acknowledged value you contribute. When it comes to growth in life, a positive personal brand is crucial. Leaders tend to consider people with positive personal brands to tap for a role or trust with a major account.

You must be able to communicate your values to a leader - what can you deliver that others can't? I call this your USP (Unique Selling Preposition).

The path to sponsorship discovery involves a series of steps. Essentially, you must believe in this immutable principle of human existence as it governs the affairs of men. You must realise that life's success is not only a determinant of the most skilled, most talented and most hard working, but time and chance happen to men.

It takes a lot of effort and focus to tap into this principle. The following are the key steps to observe:

- Diligence

- Consistency

- Passion

- Great belief system

- Acquisition of the right set of skills

- Unique selling preposition

- Be prepared to be alone

- Ability to swallow criticisms

- Constant self-improvement/evaluation

- Humility

- Don't be in a hurry

- Go for the small things people generally despise

- Patience

In attracting the right sponsorship, you must be painstaking in your daily life pursuit.

In attracting the right sponsorship, you must be painstaking in your daily life pursuit. The bible says any man diligent in his ways will stand before kings and nobles and not ordinary men. The more you engage a process, the better are the chances that you will keep improving.

Do not be weary in doing well, for in due season you will reap if you faint not. The battle of life is not for the faint hearted. I remembered vividly in the early part of my life as young man growing up in the city of Abuja.

Precisely in the year 2003, this was three years after my employment at my current place of work. I decided to take a giant leap of faith and made a bold move to own a house of mine. That year, during the summer holiday, I gathered all the funds I had and paid for a family holiday for my wife and our two children to the United Kingdom.

Few days after they left, one fateful morning while going through the daily newspapers, I came across an advert of a developer building a housing estate, somewhere in the Katampe District of Abuja. It was an estate comprising of units of 2 and 3 bedrooms and some units of semi-detached duplexes.

I decided to go for the 2-bedroom unit as a young growing man; it was simply a leap of faith, I did not have the money in my account. The cost of the unit was going for a couple of millions, but I absolutely did not even have one hundred thousand naira.

> *My proposed six-month plan sounded not plausible, but guess what, immediately I made that move, the estate developer approved my request. This was the first testimony, and with that I was emboldened to press on.*

But one thing I knew was that my heart was settled about that property. The first step of faith I took was to initiate a negotiation with the developer. On the newspaper advert was a demand for two-month payment, but I decided to push for a six-month payment plan.

My proposed six-month plan sounded not plausible, but guess what, immediately I made that move, the estate developer approved my request. This was the first testimony, and with that I was emboldened to press on.

Over the next five months I was able to make payments, amounting to some millions, which translated to about 50 percent of the total cost of the home. I guess you would think I was on my way to becoming a landlord, but wait to read the series of events leading to my dream coming true.

At the sixth and final month of payment for that property I became due for a home ownership program in my place of work. I subsequently applied and the processing was on, the amount expected would be enough to settle the outstanding payment to the developer.

All seems good, I had gotten confirmation from my HR department that my account would be credited, so we began preparations to move to our new home, I informed my landlord we were moving out, and in fact a new tenant had come to take a look at my apartment preparatory to moving in. Just then the impossible happened.

I recall one thing kept going through my mind and my speech was there is no aborted project with God; my confession was He that has started this good work will see to its finish. I told my wife I would not ask for equity refund and that we will move into the home, whether the enemy liked it or not.

One fateful morning, after I had taken some days off to enable me focus on the move, I got this call from my HR department that the account department had noticed an anomaly and that I was not due for the payment until another 12 months and they were sorry for any inconveniences.

This news was like a thunderbolt; the dream of moving into our new home seemed about to be aborted. I called up my wife and broke the news to her; we were both in shock, as we did not know how to proceed. Lots of options were running through our heads, one of the most feasible was to abort the project, take back equity contribution and wait for another year to try again as the developer was not willing to accommodate an extension.

I recall one thing kept going through my

mind and my speech was there is no aborted project with God; my confession was He that has started this good work will see to its finish. I told my wife I would not ask for equity refund and that we will move into the home, whether the enemy liked it or not.

That same day, after some hours of allowing the news to settle in, I picked up my car key and told my wife I needed to take a drive. She was a bit worried as she was not sure of my state of mind at this point. I drove out but less than 10 minutes after I took that drive, I looked to my left side and I saw a billboard of a mortgage home financing company, something in me said 'stop and go into that office.'

> *I needed to take that step of*
> *faith, which God honoured, and*
> *brought people who I had never*
> *met in my life prior to that day*
> *to help actualise my dream.*

I drove into the office and walked to the reception and thereafter I asked to see the Managing Director. I filled the visitors form and after some waiting I was ushered into his presence by the secretary. I introduced myself and looked into the managing director's face and said I want money to complete the payment of my dream home.

The MD looked into my eyes and said 'young man we don't give money to people to go buy houses, in fact we have our projects as we are into real estates and this office was set up to help people who want to buy any of our property, you are not buying from us and as such I cannot help you.'

I persisted, and told him, 'sir, I know some of your projects but I'm really not interested in any of them, I have identified what I want and need you to close the deal for me.' When he saw my persistence, he told me I should put down my request in writing and that the only person with the power to grant such a waiver was the chairman of the company. He was not making any promise, but he would discuss my request and make a case for me before the chairman and that I should return the following day for feedback.

I left his office and went home and told my wife of my adventure, she was perplexed, but I recalled that I told her that for my sake protocol would be broken. The night was very long. The following day, I woke up, got dressed and went back to the office. Guess what happened when I arrived the MD's office, he paused for a while and looked into my eyes and then said 'young man, I don't know what happened, but the chairman approved and requested we disburse the money to you.'

Daily in life we are faced with situations that would test our faith, diligence, perseverance, and consistency of purpose. We need to be prepared to push to that finishing line. God is always constant and faithful, only if we dare to believe and His word says 'prove ye me this day, if I will not open the windows of heaven and pour blessings on you, beyond your imagination.'

This was the testimony to owning our first home in Abuja. We eventually paid and moved in and twelve months after that we completely paid off what we borrowed from the firm.

This is a classical illustration of sponsorship at play, as there was no way for the MD to have advocated for me if I stayed back groping and sulking on how unfair my company was to me in denying me those funds at the last moment. I needed to take that step of faith, which God honoured, and brought people who I had never met in my life prior to that day to help actualise my dream.

Daily in life we are faced with situations that would test our faith, diligence, perseverance, and consistency of purpose. We need to be prepared to push to that finishing line. God is always constant and faithful, only if we dare to believe and His word says 'prove ye me this day, if I will not open the windows of heaven and pour blessings on you, beyond your imagination.'

My dear reader, you cannot wish away this principle, whether you like it or not, this is how the world operates. God Almighty knew the efficacy of this principle, such that Jesus needed to be borne by a woman into this world. Even though God had the sovereign power, Jesus did not evolve. God is a God of order.

> *This man lacked a sponsor, yearly he waited for a sponsor and none came, until one day Jesus saw him and asked him, son of man would you be made whole, his response was very instructive, I don't have any man to help, meaning 'I do not have a sponsor.*

God knew Jesus needed a sponsor, so John the Baptist had to be conceived six (6) months before Mary took in. Read the account of John the Baptist: the sole purpose he was born was to introduce, set the scene and herald the coming of Christ. He knew his time was up immediately Jesus was revealed, no wonder he echoed, 'He will increase and I will decrease.'

The sponsorship of Jesus by John started even before their births. The bible reveals that six months into the conception of John; Mary visited Elizabeth and the account was that the baby in her womb lifted up for joy. John was already excited about Jesus even before birth. Don't hang around people who are not excited about you whether you are there or not. You can not sponsor what you are not excited about.

The law of gravitation says any object that goes up must come down due to the force of gravity; that law can't be broken. The only modification to that law is the theory of aerodynamics, this law has been able to temporarily suspend the gravity law, but unable to invalidate it. This is why aircraft can go up so high into the sky, fly thousands of miles carrying so much weight of people and materials, but eventually it does not stay up forever, it still comes down to earth, in fulfilment of the law of gravity.

This was exactly what the blind man by the sheep gate pool (John 5: 1-15) was taking about. He had been by that pool for close to 40 years and every year, we are told, an angel comes to stir the pool and anyone who is the first to jump into it is healed of whatsoever infirmity he or she had.

This man lacked a sponsor. Yearly he waited for a sponsor and none came, until one day Jesus saw him and asked him, son of man would you be made whole? His response was very instructive, I don't have any man to help, meaning 'I do not have a sponsor.' Jesus told him, yes, I know you do not have a sponsor, but I have come today as your sponsor, I am breaking that chain, pick up your bed, go home and you are made whole. That same hour, the blind man picked up his bed and went home healed.

The force of the principle of sponsorship held this blind man bound for close to 40 years; guess what, help was not in sight and God knew that if no sponsor showed up this man would most likely die there. Jesus had to show up as his sponsor.

The force of the principle of sponsorship held this blind man bound for close to 40 years; guess what, help was not in sight and God knew that if no sponsor showed up this man would most likely die there. Jesus had to show up as his sponsor.

6

FINAL
THOUGHTS
CALL TO ACTION

I have told my story and shared my thoughts in this book as openly and honestly as I can. I hope that after reading you will be inspired to do the right thing and take action.

Change can only take place by doing, not by inaction. The potent force of sponsorship has been my story all the way. At every point in my life, God has always brought sponsors my way and, guess what, it did not just happen by chance. I needed to be sensitive to realize it, when critical people came my path.

I recalled working with a colleague, years ago. This great guy joined my present place of work from abroad. But we struck a bond, I made myself useful in helping him settle down into the company and as time moved on the relationship grew stronger.

About a year after he joined our

establishment, one day he came to my office and told me to go pick up a land application form at the federal capital territory. This was during the tenure of Mallam Nasir el-Rufai as the FCT Minister, sanity was being brought to the land allocation system and ordinary people could actually apply for land and be given.

Based on my friend's prompting, I went ahead and purchased the application form for the sum of N50, 000 and submitted the form. Other colleagues in my office also applied for land too, so I was not the only person. I guess you will be wondering in your mind what next. Few months after that application, I was allocated a land in one of the satellite towns in Abuja, Kubwa to be precise.

I recall vividly that something happened weeks after the allocation when I had not picked up the allocation letter. One morning, while we were at work, he asked if I had picked my allocation letter, my response to him was no. He was surprised and asked why. Typical of me, I told him I was not keen as the area where the land was, was not really what I had anticipated, and told him my preference would have been for a piece of land right in the heart of the city.

This was sponsorship at work. I was only the person of my colleagues who applied that had his allocation substituted. But it did not just happen; I had to demand for it. I was not scared of being labelled an ingrate, after all I had a land, millions of people were on the queue and got nothing. Don't settle for less, most times we are excited over small things when we can actually demand for more.

The next response from him was that, I should not pick up the allocation letter, and that he would see what he could do for me. Prior to joining our organization he had worked in the Federal Capital Territory ministry and knew his way around. Guess what, with that I got another allocation right in the city, just as I had desired. I went ahead, collected my allocation paper, and over the next 18 months paid for the title document.

This was sponsorship at work. I was the only person of all my colleagues who applied that had his allocation substituted. But it did not just happen; I had to demand for it. I was not scared to be labelled an ingrate, after all I had a land, millions of people were on the queue and got nothing. Don't settle for less, most times we are excited over small things when we can actually demand for more.

I can say for sure that my career has been great, but the defining moment came when a certain boss came on board. This man believed so much in me that he had to push for the impossible to have my career path changed.

Before he came, I had different supervisors, but this was the person who took out time to study my career path and was prepared to ensure that I did not settle for less. In the history of my department, I am the only person who has had the opportunity to go for an international assignment and who was not a manager; guess what, the numbers are not much, only four persons have benefitted.

In fact I was to learn later, after my return from my international assignment in the United States of America, that my then managing director actually made some push backs before granting the approval as he was not sure I could handle the rigour of that assignment. But this boss, I was to learn later, stuck his neck out for me and defended my choice for that assignment. Thank God I did not disappoint him as I delivered on that assignment. But the truth was that somebody stood up for me at the opportune time. We all need people who will believe in us and push our destiny when the opportunity comes up.

My entire life has been about sponsorship, if it worked for me it can for you. Don't go on this journey of life without a sponsor, the pains and headaches are too much to bear and it is certainly not worth it. Sponsors shorten time, distance, space and generally give you a leveraging advantage.

Made in the USA
Coppell, TX
16 July 2023

19151511R00063